God is Greater than the Ups and Downs

By: Jason Root

Contents

Introduction

My name is Jason Root, and I have lived in Manchester, Kentucky, my entire life. I was born on February 18, 1976 through the union of Robert and Barbara Ann Root. At the time of my birth, I had a five-year-old brother named Shannon. My father, Robert Root, was drafted in the Vietnam War during 1969, and came home in July of 1970. During his time of service, he was in close quarter combat and endured many horrible things that would later affect him mentally and physically. Although my father's time at war was short, he received a Purple Heart for his brave service. During my father's time in the Vietnam War, he was sprayed with a substance called Agent Orange, which was used tactically by the United States Army against the Vietnamese. Agent Orange was a harmful pesticide meant to harm the Vietnamese army, but it caused dual harm to both the Vietnamese and US soldiers. This substance greatly affected my father mentally in the short-term, and both mentally and physically in the long-term. While in Vietnam, the close quarter combat was so brutal that my father intentionally took a grenade and blew off his left arm in order to come home. Mentally, he struggled with what we know today as post-traumatic stress disorder (PTSD) and other mental health issues. The Vietnam War was brutal and my father was a culprit of both mental and physical effects of its destruction. My father died in 2007, at the age of 52, due to side effects of Agent Orange. My brother, Shannon, and I, were both born with birth defects as a result of my father's exposure to Agent Orange. Many children whose fathers were impacted by Agent Orange were also born with birth defects that would impact their quality of life. Current law only allows children who were born with certain health conditions to receive financial compensation. My brother and I were greatly impacted by Agent Orange, and we have struggled to receive any government assistance or outreach from the Veterans Affairs. My brother Shannon, and I, developed a rare eye disease called Retinitis Pigmentosa which causes blindness. My brother (who recently passed away), and I, also have many other underlying health issues and have not been able to get any form of financial help. We cannot work and are dependent on others to meet our basic needs. There are many others who are in this same situation. It saddens me not only for myself and my brother, but for all those who are silently suffering as a result of side effects of Agent Orange. Through it all, God has been my Rock, my Source of joy, and my Provider. Even though my earthly father has passed on, God has stepped in. The Bible says that God will be a father to the fatherless (Psalms 68:5), and He has never failed to provide all I need (Matthew 6:33). The purpose of this book that God has called me to write, is to share pieces of my life that have been impacted by Agent Orange while shedding light on the lack of assistance that is available to those who have been affected with lifelong health conditions. Yes, I have been negatively impacted by my father's exposure to Agent Orange, but God! The Bible says that God will give me beauty for ashes and His grace has done just that! God has taken this disability and made it a testimony to share with others about God's grace. God wants you to know that He can take something evil and turn it for your good (Romans 8:28).

Foreword

Jason Root is one of the mightiest of prayer warriors that I have ever known. I met him at my daughter's third birthday party in London, Kentucky. He came with a mutual friend, Larietta Elliott. Jason had prayed for Larietta's son, Reid, when he was hospitalized at 2-years-old. Reid received a miracle and a healing touch from God! Jason was her main source of prayer, and now he was at my daughter's third birthday party. When we were introduced, he said the Lord brought him there to pray for me because I had been diagnosed with breast cancer and was undergoing treatment at that time. Since the diagnosis, I had a newfound love for Jesus and was happy to be alive! I was amazed that God had introduced me to Jason so he could pray for me. Who am I that God would send such a prayer warrior to consistently pray for me each week and continually three years later! Since then, Jason and I have had our fair share of ups and downs, but Jason has never failed to call me each week or daily depending on the need, and pray for my family and I. He hears from the Lord and many times has called to prophecy over my life. I love it when he calls and says "The Lord laid it on my heart to call you...." then he shares with me exactly what I had been concerned about that week! It is always a right on time word that blesses me and brings me to tears. Jason is the only one that my husband, Matthew, who struggles with addiction, has opened up to because Jason has never been judgmental. Jason is always positive and encouraging, no matter what is going on in his life. Jason may be blind for this season, but God has plans to restore his vision. I know that one day Jason will experience a miracle from God, and his blind eyes will be opened to see the many people he has prayed for!

~1~ The Setup: Going off to War!

Ephesian 2:10 "For we are his workmanship, created in Christ Jesus for good works which God prepared beforehand so that we would walk in them."

My father, Robert Root was born December 22, 1947, in Manchester, Kentucky. My mother, Barbara Ann was born October 26, 1945 in Manchester as well. I was raised in a Christian home and as far as I know, so were my parents. My maternal grandfather was a Pentecostal preacher at Morgan Branch Pentecostal Church for almost 40 years. When the church first started it only seated about 30 people, and now it seats 250 people! The church has been there a long time and the Lord continues to bless it today, long after the passing of my grandfather who died in 2010. He built the church from the ground up, and it is in full operation today. He was certainly motivated by the Lord! When my grandfather was young he routinely drank alcohol and played cards, and was essentially one of the worst people in Clay County. At roughly 45-years-old, he was invited to a tent revival by my grandmother, and he gave his life to Jesus. The day following his salvation, he went to work at the coal mines and told his coworkers that if he cussed to let him know. Cussing must have been a stronghold, especially if you need a co-worker to point it out! That same day, he hit his finger with a hammer and a cuss word came out. Instead of needing a co-worker to remind him of his foul language, God spoke to him, and my grandfather asked for forgiveness. From that day forward, he never spoke another cuss word. As his grandson, fortunately I never knew the Bob Stevens that was a cussing, drunk who gambled, I only knew the preacher side of my grandfather. My grandfather could not read, but after accepting Jesus as his Savior, he began listening to an audio Bible. He heard the Lord call him to preach while listening to the Bible and was later called to preach at Morgan Branch Pentecostal Church. My father, Robert, was raised in the Baptist faith, which is quite different from the Pentecostal faith. Although my parents came from different religious denominations, they were strong in the Lord. Thankfully, my parents were Christians when they met. I am not sure how they met, but I know they dated six months before they were married. It was such a shock to their friends and family because they had only dated for a short while. They were married on June 22, 1968 at Morgan Branch Pentecostal Church in Manchester, by Lester Thompson. My mother was 22, and my father was 20-years-old at the time of their marriage. Shortly after their marriage, in December of 1969, my father was drafted into the Vietnam War. My father was roughly 5'5, slightly skinny, and surely not a man for war. He was a peaceable man, and not interested in conflict or battle. At the time of the draft, my parents went directly to an army base in Kansas. There, my father received training, vaccinations, and briefing on the war, while my mother stayed on base nearby. My mother did not enjoy that time and could not wait to come home! She was unable to go to church and she often mentioned that time away from home as a time of straying from the Lord. My mother felt out of place there and wanted to be back home where she felt comfortable. The place that my parents were staying in Kansas was so dangerous, that there were curfews in place. This was so different from living in the hills of Manchester where they lived in peace and safety.

The conflict of the Vietnam War was so intense and traumatic, that my father shot his arm off with a grenade which severed his arm in two pieces. After my father self-mutilated his arm, a man carried my father to a helicopter nearby which saved his life. By the grace of God, they found the other half of my father's arm, and it was recovered. God's will was certainly at work! My father stayed at an army base in Vietnam for about two weeks before they flew him to Kansas where he would later have a full recovery. It was when my father came home from war that our family journey with Christ began.

~2~ Coming Home After the War

John 15:13 "No greater love man have to lay his life down for his friend."

When my father first came home from war in 1969, he stayed in Kansas at an army hospital for roughly two weeks while recovering from surgery. In order to piece his arm back together, a metal plate was inserted and he wore an arm brace from that point forward. After my father was home and healed from surgery, my parents decided to have children. I was born first, then my brother, Shannon. My father's arm injury determined him disabled by the VA, however he only drew 10% of his VA pension (100.00 a month). That was not enough for living expenses for a family of four. At that time, my father had to seek employment and was able to work at a local grocery store in Manchester. He went to work at Saylor's grocery store in 1992 in the deli department. After about a year of working in the deli, he began working in the coal mines until 1993. In 1993, he injured his back while on the job and was unable to work. After his injury in the coal mines, he began flea marketing on a regular basis. At the flea market, he sold knives, clothes, caps, and Christmas trees (during that time of the year). He used his work as a way to escape the mental wounds that tormented his mind. When he was at home, all he talked about was the Vietnam War. I know that he needed a break from the reel that was playing in his mind, and work was one way to cope. This was also the time he began listening to the Bible, and it helped my mother and father change their lives. With all the hardships that would come later, they did not know exactly how much they would need Jesus going forward. I am thankful now that my father and mother were seeking the Lord and would later on, teach me how to have a relationship with Jesus.

As a child, I remember my father having frequent nightmares due to post-traumatic stress, however this occurrence became more frequent later on in life. Toward the end of his life he had several mental break-downs and had several stays in the mental ward at the VA. Some of the side effects of Agent Orange caused frail bones, heart disease, diabetes, cirrhosis of the liver, etc. all of which my father battled after coming home from war. The symptoms of post-traumatic stress became so severe that as my father aged, he chose isolation. I think he was afraid he would hurt my brother and I, or even my mother. The things my father suffered as a result of war and Agent Orange were taxing on him and my mother, especially, later on in their marriage.

Even in the midst of flashbacks and stressful situations, my father loved to fish and he did so often. He frequently stayed in a cabin on Lake Cumberland, Kentucky, to avoid being around people. At one point, he lived alone in a mobile home in London, Kentucky. He wanted to be alone and my mother, Shannon, and I understood and were considerate of his needs. Toward the end of his life, he came back to Manchester to be taken care of. The cabin and mobile home had to be sold because the symptoms of post-traumatic stress were so severe and could not be left alone. In the midst of all the ups and downs, God allowed our family to prosper and serve Him. My father did not realize at the time that God had ministry work in store for his children and that all the trails my father faced would serve a purpose later on.

~3~The First Birth

Matthew 4: 18-20, "As Jesus was walking beside the Sea of Galilee, he saw two brothers, Simon called Peter and his brother Andrew. They were casting a net into the lake, for they were fishermen. "Come, follow me,"Jesus said,"and I will send you out to fish for people."At once they left their nets and followed him."

During the good years of my mother and father's marriage, they decided to have children. The first born was me, Robert Shannon Root, on July 27, 1971. Shannon was born with Retinitis Pigmentosa and began wearing glasses at 5-years-old. With glasses, Shannon had 20/20 vision. As a small child, Shannon also had problems with the development of his feet. In fact, the doctor told my mother that he would never walk, but God had a different plan! In addition to being born with Retinitis Pigmentosa and developmental delays, Shannon was born with cirrhosis of the liver. We did not find out he had cirrhosis of the liver until he was 41-years-old. As a small child, Shannon's night vision was poor and physical and mental developments were delayed, but God sustained him and allowed him to have a very normal childhood. Shannon's night vision was so bad from the eye disease that at church one night, he fell off the steps of the church house and fractured his leg! Shannon bounced back quickly and he moved on from that incident!

Shannon and I were both raised in church. Shannon gave his life to the Lord in 1992, at 21-years-old. Shannon liked fishing and sporting events. He often played basketball and hung out at Beach Creek lake with his friends. Although Shannon's vision was deteriorating, that did not stop him from doing things he loved. Doctors told my mother when Shannon was born, that he had "mental retardation," and would require special education all throughout his time in school. When Shannon's vision was closer to 20/20, he could read some, however, his vision hindered him from doing much reading most of the time. During elementary school, my mother was a cook in the cafeteria. She took the position to be close to Shannon because of his disabilities. She cooked in the cafeteria for nine years, and then cooked as a substitute at the high school for four years. Shannon stayed in special education classes the entirety of his schooling. Shannon did not like school, but he went because he had to. Shannon went to the vocational school as a senior in high school and he did carpentry work. Shannon seemed to enjoy working with his hands and had great potential to be a real carpenter had his vision not deteriorated. Unfortunately, Shannon has never driven a car or been employed. In 2006, Shannon went fully blind from Retinitis Pigmentosa at the age of 35. Shannon's vision got progressively worse as life went on, and then one day, he woke-up blind. Because he had worn glasses for so long, he continued to wear them after going blind. Shannon had worn glasses for many years and it seemed to provide him with some peace. Shannon became depressed about a year after going blind. He was encouraged to continue doing the things he loved in order to help keep his mind off the rapid changes that were taking place. Shannon continued to go fishing, even though he required assistance, he still managed to still catch some fish. Shannon caught some large fish that my mother had mounted. Shannon did not let this disability keep him from living his life! Overtime, the cirrhosis of the liver hindered Shannon from being able to fish for long periods of time, and eventually he stopped fishing altogether. At age 46, Shannon was called into ministry by calling and praying with people over the phone. Shannon would call people that he knew were sick, and would ask if he could pray for them. Shannon desired to call people who were sickly so often, that Shannon knew that God had called him into this ministry! Shannon would pray for people that went to our church, and would often speak at their funerals. Throughout Shannon's life, he attended Morgan Branch Pentecostal Church, Jack's Branch Bible Church, and New Beginning Community Church, all in Manchester, Kentucky. Shannon's favorite Bible verse is John 3:16 and he could quote it well!

~4~The Second Birth

Proverbs 3:5 "Trust in the Lord with all your heart and lean not on your own understanding."

I was born February 18, 1976. My mother was 30-years-old, my father was 28-years-old, and Shannon was 5-years-old at the time of my birth. When I was three months old, my mother and uncle were at home playing cards when I began convulsing and stopped breathing. My mother immediately began praying for the Lord to spare my life! God did, and my mother rededicated her life and decided she would serve him for the rest of hers! She was sold out for the Lord because of His Divine touch in that moment that saved my life! When I was young, I used to play Nintendo and was really good at it. My favorite games were Donkey Kong, Mario Brothers and Pac-Man. My brother and I would often play video games together. I also enjoyed playing video games with my mother. I started elementary school at 5-years old at Manchester Elementary and went there through the 8th grade. I went to high school at Clay County High School. When I graduated from high school, I was 40th in my class. I graduated from high school in 1995, at the age of 18. At the age of ten, I gave my life to the Lord at Morgan Branch Pentecostal Church. There was a revival at the church, and the preacher gave a sermon on hell. I was afraid to go to the altar and pray, so I prayed at home that night with my parents. The Spirit of God was on me that night and I began praying the sinner's prayer, " Jesus, I am a sinner please come into my heart and save me!" and He did. Shortly after I decided to follow Jesus, my grandfather baptized me a few weeks later. This baptism was an unusual experience. My grandfather held me underwater for so long (at least several minutes as I recall) that following the baptism, I was scared of water for several weeks. He said the reason he held me under so long was for the salvation to stick! That was enough for it to stick alright! I went to church every time the doors were open at Morgan Branch Pentecostal Church from that point on.

When I was a freshman in high school, someone I trusted dearly, let me down and I ended up straying from the Lord. During that time, I only went to church on Sunday mornings for several years. After church on Sunday mornings, we would visit my paternal grandmother in the nursing home in Hyden, Kentucky. Because of our visits to Hyden on Sunday's, I would often become tired and used that as an excuse to get out of church on Sunday nights. Of course I could no longer use that as an excuse after she died. During this same time, my cousin and her husband invited me to church with them on a Sunday night in the summer of 1993. I was 17 at the time, slacking in my relationship with Jesus, and I decided to rededicate my life to the Lord.

During elementary and high school, I went to all the sporting events and enjoyed it greatly. My favorite sport was basketball. My father, my brother, and myself, attended every basketball game from 1991-1995. Unfortunately, Clay County schools never won a state championship, but I did enjoy the time with my father and brother and wouldn't trade it for nothing. During grade school, I chased girls quite often. I had two girl-friends in elementary school that I really liked. In high school, I met a cheerleader named Kay Jones. She and I became very close friends while in high school and we are still great friends today. Kay assists me with my podcast and with any technology issues I may have. While in high school, a young lady named Marketa died in a car crash. I will never forget going to school that day and asking where she was, and being told she was killed in a car accident. It really crushed me! She sat behind me in one of my classes and I considered her a good friend. It devastated me because I had never known anyone so young to die.

My relationship with my parents was good. We enjoyed watching wrestling and the Atlanta Braves together. We had a tradition to go out to eat on Friday nights before church, then we would go to Walmart. My mother always wanted to rush home to watch Dallas at 10 PM! For vacation, we would always go to Pigeon Forge and stay several days. We always looked forward to our family vacations each year.

When I was 16-years-old, my father started having intense nightmares. He would often get up and attempt to fight and cuss my mother and I. He was a great Christian man, however he was experiencing symptoms of PTSD that were threatening and dangerous. This would happen every few nights, and to the point where I was afraid to go to sleep. It was so severe that I was scared to come out

of my room for fear of him attacking me. I knew he could not control these events, and I loved him

anyway. In October 1994, at 18, my great uncle, Jeff Stevens, built me the house that I live in now. This

became a safe space to be away from my father. That small house became my home and I still live

there today. The house I live in today is right next door to the home I grew up in. It is a blessing to still

live in my neighborhood around family who now help me everyday.

~5~ The Diagnosis

Romans 8:28 "And we know that all things work together for good to them that love God, to them who are called according to His purpose."

I was diagnosed with Retinitis Pigmentosa at 5-years-old by an optometrist named Teresa Madden. I was her first patient that she ever treated with this particular eye disease. Although I had 20/20 vision with prescription glasses, little did I know that I would lose total vision later in life. Dr. Madden wrote in her medical files that the disease I had was a result of my father's exposure to Agent Orange during the Vietnam War. She knew what the disease was from just by looking into my eyes. Apparently, she had seen this disease in other people and knew where it generated from. By the 7th grade, I had to move to the front of the class in order to see the chalkboard. My vision was deteriorating, but at that time my life was full of joy and peace. In the 8th grade I went on a field trip to Dollywood and walked around the entire park by myself! During middle school, was when I began to notice that my vision was worsening. It was becoming more difficult to see, even with glasses. My freshman year of high school, I was playing basketball with some friends and was hit in the eye by accident. Consequently, my glasses broke and I went back to Dr. Teresa. It was at this time she told me my vision had gone to 2100, which is not good. I became mad at God! I did not want my vision to get worse. I wanted my life to go the way I wanted without any stumbling blocks. As I went through high school, I could not see the chalkboard, but I had an aide who would help me write down the information and enlarge the words in big print. That helped me to learn without any setbacks. If it had not been for enlarging fine print, I would have struggled to learn. In 1995, my vision went to 2800, which meant that it was very difficult for me to see. With glasses, it was difficult to see without things being enlarged. At the time when my vision went to 2800, I loved to read and collect sports cards, so my mother bought me a magnifier to be able to continue those hobbies. I wanted to drive, however when I was 16-years-old, I was told that my vision was too poor to ever be able to drive. That was heart-breaking. Like all 16-year-olds, I wanted to drive my own car and have the independence and freedom that came with it. With all the rapid changes taking place, I would go to church and just sit in the back. I listened during church, but did not pray and did not consider myself spiritual. I became depressed and was really mad at God. On September 11, 2001, I had a horrible headache. I remember watching the events of the Twin Towers and by that night, my head began to hurt. The next day the headache was still intense and I woke up and could no longer see. Everything was unusually dark and I could not see anything! It was on that day that my mother took me to the doctor, and we were told that there was nothing that could be done. The RP had eaten away at the rods in my eyes and that was what caused the blindness. I knew that my vision was getting worse, but I did not think that I was actually going blind. My doctor had not informed me that I was going blind, so it was shocking and depressing once it happened. I laid in bed for several days. I was mourning the life I had and a future of dreams that now seemed impossible. My mother decided that she was going to get a hold of Jesus! She would not accept me being depressed and grieving. One night she came over to my house, crawled on top of me and cried out to God for an hour-and-a-half. What my mother did to revive my spirit was similar to what Prophet Elijah did for the widow's son who had died in 1 Kings verses 17-24. According to that scripture, after Elijah cried out to God and he had laid on the child, life entered in him and the child was revived. Thankfully, God moved and heard the cries of my mother! I received everything that Jesus had for me that night in September. God delivered me from depression that night and I have not dealt with it again! God took something bad and gave me something good! I can go back to that day that my mother crawled on top of me and prayed for me, and remember the desperation in her voice! Sometimes it takes desperation before God will move in a situation, and I am thankful that my mother was to that point. Although the diagnosis was bad, God was better! God had a plan. This time of my life was similar to the story of Jacob who wrestled with God until God blessed him (Genesis 32:22-32). Sometimes you have to labor in prayer until God moves. My mother did just that, I am blessed to no longer feel depressed or sad about the diagnosis. Blindness has gotten easier over time as God has given me peace and a new way of living. The world could not give me peace. The peace I had only came from Jesus.

In 2016, my brother and I went to West Virginia to a doctor that was a micro acupuncture specialist that supposedly had a cure for this eye disease. The treatment was micro-acupuncture and required putting needles in our hands and feet for five days for 8 hours each day. Of course, this did not work, and God knew that it wouldn't work. At the time of our treatment, the doctor who was performing the acupuncture had been diagnosed with cancer. So, I prayed with this man each day for five days. I was able to witness the love of Jesus to this doctor. The reason for me being there was not for me to get 20/20 vision, but for that man to receive Jesus as his Savior. It was very important for us to go to West Virginia to witness to this doctor, or otherwise he may have never known Jesus and believed the gospel. Two months after our treatment, the doctor's nurse called to let me know that he had passed away and how important it was for us to have been there to pray! God knows what He is doing, even if it involves acupuncture!

There are many lifestyle changes that I have endured since being blind. I was used to living a certain way one day, then suddenly, I had to live differently. Shortly after losing my vision, a woman from the Clay County Health Department tried to teach my brother and I to walk with a cane, but that was too difficult. It is way easier to walk holding onto someone's shoulder. Since being blind, I have had to learn to depend on people more, swallow pride, and reach out to friends and loved ones to help me with things that I cannot do on my own. My other senses are extremely heightened since losing my vision. I can hear and smell better now than I ever did before! When I go somewhere with steps, as I am being led up each stair, I feel how they are stepping and know how to adjust my steps to match theirs. When I sit down at a table to eat, I need someone to tell me where my food is and I am able to eat with my hands. I can also use a spoon or fork to know where different foods are on my plate. Depending on what I am eating, it might get messy, but I do a pretty good job at avoiding stains. It is also helpful to have someone say, "The chicken is at the top, and the beans are at the bottom." Some foods are harder to eat, especially softer foods like mashed potatoes. It takes me a while to eat those foods because I try to keep them from getting all over me. When getting dressed, my mother or my aunt Faye lays my clothes on my bed and I put them on myself. I rarely run into things in my house. I had 2100 vision at the time it was built so I am familiar with the layout of the rooms. I do not cook at all. Someone tried to help me learn how to cook one time, but it was hard to learn and quite dangerous! Because I became blind at an older age, it has become more difficult to adjust, rather than had I been blind from birth. When I go to sit down at an unknown place, I hold on to the back of the chair to keep it from moving so I know where the bottom of the chair is. I have never fallen, but I have had a chair fall over while sitting in it. Not sure what made that happen, but I was not injured as a result! Praise the Lord! Had I not become blind, I would not have had the closeness with God that I do now. This process has gotten me closer to God than what I ever thought! I am dependent on God for all my needs and He always sends me the right people to help out.

~6~ Finding Jesus

Luke 15:24 "For this my son was dead, and is alive again; he was lost and is found. And they began to be merry."

In life, there are times that we are not what God would have us to be, and we can stray from His will. In 1994, when I was 18-years-old, I got involved in things that I should not have been involved in as a Christian. I had 2100 vision at that time, which was decent. I allowed the devil to steer me in the wrong direction. I went to church every time the doors were open, even though I was back-sliding from the Lord. The Lord would knock on my heart and convict me of the things I was doing, but I did not pray and repent. The Lord has always moved on me in my home, more than in any church service. To be delivered from the sin I was in bondage to, I prayed for 30 days! Each day that I prayed, I was that much closer to being delivered. Finally, He delivered me! God had removed the thoughts and the desire was no longer there! God had a reason for allowing me to do the things I did. He did not like them, but He uses all things for His glory. When I talk to people who have struggled with addiction to drugs and alcohol, they can relate to me when I share my testimony about the bondage God delivered me from. The Bible says in James 4:8, that if we draw nigh to Him, He draws nigh unto us. I had to draw nigh to Him, before I could ever be delivered.

During the time of back-sliding, I was around the wrong people, particularly women. I became addicted to pornography for about a year. Because I had purchased pornographic videos, a bill came in the mail that ousted my secret sin. I was afraid to tell my mother, because I was afraid of how she would respond. I did not want her to think bad of me or judge me. I looked up to my mother and I did not want to disappoint her. She asked me if someone was talking me into watching these pornographic videos, but the answer was no. I chose to watch them on my own and I knew what I was doing was wrong. If we live in sin today, it is because we chose to do so. God wants us to live for Him and live a holy life (1 Peter 1:15). No matter what people are going through, the Lord can help us get through it! Sometimes it's hard to go back and think of the things that we have done in our lives, especially those things that are embarrassing and sinful. The pornographic addiction began as a result of lusting after women. The women I was talking to and being around at that time, were not Christian women. However, the choices were my own. I blame myself, not God for what I was involved in. I allowed the devil to come in. The Bible says that the Joy of the Lord is my strength (Nehemiah) and I would need the Joy of the Lord to help me overcome the lies of the devil! I allowed the devil to steal my joy for a season, but the Lord restored my Joy and I am thankful! The Bible says to not look to the left or the right, but to focus on Jesus (Proverbs 4:25-27).

God can deliver you from anything you are dealing with if you will allow God to move. I was ashamed when my mother found out I had been watching pornographic videos. I thought she would hate me and be mad at me. Thankfully, when I told her that God had delivered me and forgiven me, my mother hugged me and said she did too. After being delivered from this addiction, I was closer to God and focused on Him more. Even though I was saved during that time of back-sliding, God never gave up on me and I am now free from that form of bondage.

God also delivered me from a crutch of wearing glasses. I began wearing glasses when I was five-years-old. At a preaching commitment one night at Macedonia Baptist church in Manchester, God laid it on my heart to preach about laying crutches down in our lives. I told the congregation that I had been carrying a crutch of wearing glasses, even though they did not help me. From that day forward, I told them I was never going to wear glasses again, and I haven't since that very day. God can deliver us from the big things and the little things. All we have to do is trust in Him.

~7~A Time of Peace

Luke 17:19 "And he said unto him, Arise, go thy way: thy faith had made thee whole."

There was a five year window that I considered to be a time of peace in my life. It was the 1980's. I was about 10-years-old when it began. A time that all needs were met. During these five years of my life, I was going to church and school and had no problems in my life. Everything was easy in life during this time. I was a church-goer, but never read the Bible and rarely prayed. I was a bit too immersed in the things of the world, yet during this time God allowed me to build friendships, enjoy sporting events, and to smoothly transition into high school. With glasses, I had 20/20 vision at this time, and all was good. Everything was great from my perspective. Although I did not appreciate God the way I should have, He allowed me a season to grow-up into the young man I have become. Little did I know that this was the calm before the storm. I should have thanked God more often for what I had. No family members died or tragedies happened during that time. My parents were financially stable. My father worked in the coal mines and my mother worked as a cook. It was the most peaceful five years of my life. I had no needs either. If I wanted or needed anything, my parents got it for me. I made straight A's in school. I am thankful now for that time period.

I have to point out that during the 1980's the Bible was allowed in schools, and we had prayer before lunch. I am thankful all this was allowed, but I never really took it to heart the way I should have. Now, since these are not allowed, I see the difference in the quality of education that children are now receiving and how it's impacted their spirituality. I appreciate the atmosphere I grew up in that supported Godly things.

~8~ The Trials

James 1:2-4 "(2) My brethren, count it all joy when ye fall into divers temptations; (3) Knowing this, that the trying of your faith worketh patience. (4) But let patience have her perfect work, that ye may be perfect and entire, wanting nothing."

In life, things sometimes go the way we think, and other times not. When I turned 16 years old, I wanted my vision to be good enough to drive a car. At that time I had 20/40 vision with glasses, so I went to the courthouse to take the test for my permit. It was a written test and prior to taking the written test, an eye exam was required. I failed the eye exam and unfortunately never got to take the written exam. The lady was nice about it, but it still crushed me. I was so discouraged, I cried. It was hard, but I had to accept that driving was not in God's plan for me. During the mid 90's, I completed high school and graduated 40th in my class of 220 people. I really thought I would be an accountant because God blessed me to be good with numbers. I received the math award in 1995 and just knew I had a bright future to be successful. In fact, people copied my math work because I was so good at it! I am not condoning cheating at all, but I also understand that not everyone is good at math either. Two of the young men that I was friends with in high school are now preachers in local churches in Manchester, Kentucky. One of those men always joked with me that he was one of those who copied off me to help him pass! Little did I know, God was using our friendship to bless him later on in life. I introduced this man to his lovely wife, and he now pastors a local church.

Upon graduating, I really wanted to be an accountant. Numbers meant math and money to me, and had nothing to do with God. Math was something that I learned, and thought I would make a living at. Again, God was not in the numbers, how could He be? To me, math was learned, not an anointing from the Lord. During the summer of 1995, I had continual headaches for almost a month, and could not get out of bed. My vision was getting worse by the day. I began to seek the Lord and prayed to Him, asking, "Why am I going through this?" God replied to my heart, "You don't know the big picture I have for your life. It will be put together." After He spoke that to my heart, the headaches ceased. The headaches could have been from stress or other things going on in my life, either way, God took them from me. Only God knows our future. Proverbs 3 says, "If we acknowledge the Lord in all our ways He will make our path straight." God had to put me in a bed for thirty days with a terrible headache for me to accept that I was not going to become an accountant. God knew ahead of time what He had in store for me. Although I could not see the plans God had for me, I knew deep in my heart to trust Him. I knew He had brought me this far, and He was not going to fail me now! God knew that I was acknowledging Him like never before, and He has since directed my steps. Today, I am still good with numbers. In my mind I have a rolodex of many peoples phone numbers and addresses. I have around 1,000 phone numbers memorized as of writing this book. God certainly had a plan for my talent with numbers, just not in the way I thought!! As a prayer warrior, I reach out to those 1,000 individuals at least once a month, to see if there is anything I can help them with.

~9~ The Real Plan Begins

Jeremiah 29:11 "For I know the thoughts that I think toward you, saith the Lord, thoughts of peace, not of evil, to give you an expected end."

God has a plan for our lives. Even when we do not know what those plans look like, His plan is always best, and far exceeds what we could ever plan ourselves. When I was in school, I thought I was going to drive, become an accountant, and be independent. God had a different plan! God needed me to be good with numbers because He needed me to memorize phone numbers and addresses for ministry work. God was going to call me into praying for people over the phone, and I would need to have a mental system for memorizing numbers. In 1995, my mother bought me a magnifier that cost $2500. I planned on using it to look at baseball cards, but God had a different plan. It was after high school that I started wanting to know more about the Lord. At church, they handed out "Daily Bread" devotionals which consisted of a memory verse and devotion for each day. They were encouraging, so I began memorizing the daily Bible verses using the magnifier that my mother had purchased. I had no intention of using the magnifier to memorize Bible verses, I thought I would be looking at baseball cards!! But, God had a different plan.

In 2001, I was 25-years-old, and had settled into life with blind eyes and a fresh calling from the Lord. I had a talent for numbers and nothing yet to do with it. It was at a rally and fundraiser for George W. Bush in London, Kentucky, that would seal my calling in the phone ministry. My aunt and cousin made it to meet him, but my mother and I did not. That was the day I passed out! No prior warning either. I just hit the ground. A man in a suit and tie got down on his hands and knees and prayed over me after I passed out. After his prayer, I woke up lying on the ground. It was a miracle that I did not harm myself when I fell, considering that I landed on concrete. Thankfully, it was not a heart problem, but my thyroid, which was removed 14 years later in 2015. He prayed over me, and then called an ambulance. The ambulance got me to the hospital in 8 minutes and my mother left my aunt and cousin to catch a ride in a police car to the hospital. It was a few weeks after I collapsed that God called me into the phone ministry. I believe God used that moment to activate me into my calling. God does not let a crisis go bad and he used it for my good.

In 2006, most of the churches in Manchester began hosting a county-wide Vacation Bible School. This lasted until 2010. If you're not familiar with a county-wide Bible school, it entails churches coming together to host one Bible school event, instead of each church hosting them individually. It cut costs and seemed practical. In the summer of 2007, I helped with the teens and would pray with them. During one of the evenings of Bible school, I heard a man give his testimony and the Lord spoke to my heart and said, "I have blessed you and it's time to start using the knowledge that I have given you from the Daily Bread to tell others about me. I have given you a testimony!" My response to God was, "I will when I am ready." After listening to this man's testimony, he came up to me and asked me if I would come to his tent meeting and testify. I told him I would call him. I originally had no plans of calling him, but God sure did. God held me to my word. In August of 2007, I went to the Baptist Jubilee, which was a three night revival at Horse Creek Baptist church. One night during the revival, God began speaking to my heart. I knew God was calling me to be a minister and I had two ways it was going to become a reality: the hard way or the easy way. I told God that night that I was tired of doing things my way and wanted the easy way out this time. I promised Him I would go anywhere, any time to do His work, and I have ever since that night. In 2012, He called me in the radio and nursing home ministries. I have done jail ministry several times, not weekly, but sporadically as God would have me to. In 2020, God called me in the podcast ministry, with the help of a dear friend. In 2020, God also called me into the cross mailing ministry. I began Facebook Live ministry this past year, in 2022. In the beginning of 2020, I was at a church and a lady gave me a box full of metal crosses, and told me to hand them out to people. It was easy to give them out for a while, then COVID hit. During COVID and beyond, I began mailing the crosses along with my testimony, and any other small items to people that the Lord lays on my heart. These crosses have blessed so many people far and wide!

In 2011, God spoke to my heart about calling a certain preacher in Middlesboro, Kentucky, that pastors a very large, well-known church. I had heard that this pastor's son had cancer, and God wanted me to pray for the pastor to get through this trying season. I told the Lord that I did not have this pastor's phone number. Deep down I did not want to call him, because I felt intimidated. How was I going to call and pray with such a well-known pastor? What if, when I called him, he told me no? What if he said I was crazy for calling him out of the blue to pray with him? I told my aunt Joan about what God had laid on my heart, and she said that she listened to that preacher every week. She even knew how to get his phone number because it was displayed on the screen during the online church service. Needless to say, I had no excuse for not calling him. I told God I would call this preacher early in the morning on the upcoming Sunday. I figured he would be busy preparing his sermon and Sunday school lesson, and not answer. To my surprise, he answered on the first ring! I told him who I was and what God wanted me to do for him. This pastor said that it blessed him, and he wanted me to call him every Sunday until God healed his son from cancer! After this pastor's son was healed (and of course he was healed, we serve an awesome God), I was invited to this pastor's church to give my testimony. It was during my visit that I met the pastor's brother, Gary. While there, I gave my testimony five different times to over 850 people. I was so nervous. It was on a Wednesday night, and I thought there would not be that many people there. I had no idea I would be ministering to this many people! It was such a blessing to speak to that many people and testify about what God has done in my life. Now, this pastor and his whole family and I are friends. Later on, Gary, the pastor's brother and Sunday school teacher, found out he had the same exact eye disease as my brother and I. He is now fully blind, and I call him every Saturday to pray with him. This man was born with this disease, but was not a result of Agent Orange. I was blessed to meet with Gary at a 3-day revival in 2004, on the very day he was diagnosed with this disease. It was almost ten years later before he went blind in 2014. It was in 2014 when God placed this man back in my life. God sure does have a way of putting people in and out of our lives in just the right time. I am blessed to have known so many people who are strong in the Lord.

I have led many people to the Lord. In 2018, I prayed with 150 people that decided to give their lives to the Lord. After COVID, it became difficult to have access to people to minister to. Even now, the in-person church attendance has significantly declined, while online church services have soared.

My mother was one of my best prayer partners. My mother and I prayed together every morning for the last 15 years. During COVID, my mother and I would watch church on Facebook Live and it drew us close with one another. I am thankful that the online church served its intended purpose for a season, and now I am blessed to be back in church every Sunday fellow-shipping with people.

~10~ The Testimonies

Isaiah 55:8-9 "For my thoughts are not your thoughts, neither are my ways your ways, saith the Lord. For as the heavens are higher than the earth, so are my ways higher than your ways, and my thoughts than your thoughts."

Revelation 12:11 "And they overcame him by the blood of the Lamb and the word of their testimony; and they loved not their lives unto death"

As a minister and an intercessor, God will bless you to pray for a lot of people. Sometimes as you pray, like in Matthew 7:7 (asking, seeking, and knocking) God will move for that person almost immediately. Then, other times when I pray for people, things will go the complete opposite of what you're praying! In those times, you have to have faith in God and know that He knows better, and He is answering the prayer in the best way. We pray in the best way we know how. Jesus is seated at the right hand of God and He intercepts our prayers and takes them to the Father where it's perfected. Then, it is answered in the best way, and not our way. In Romans 8:26 it says that we do not know what we ought to pray and that 'ought' allows God to move in our prayers and answer them according to His will for our lives. God answers every prayer we pray. Sometimes the exact way we want it, and other times not. Below are some testimonies of individuals that I have prayed with and for over the years. Some of these testimonies are their actual written testimonies and some are to the best of my memory. I only use their first names to respect their privacy, and have their permission to share their story with you (the reader). I pray their testimonies build your faith the way they have mine.

SHELBY: I met Shelby through my friend Lisa. Lisa's daughter played softball on the same team as Shelby. Lisa would take me to all the softball games, and I began to pray for the team prior to their games. In 2013, when Shelby was in the 6th grade, Lisa and I began sitting next to Shelby's mother during softball games and we naturally became friends. That was my foot-in-the-door to minister to Shelby. The softball team was also really good. From 6-12th grade, I followed their softball team all around the state and enjoyed watching them play. I was able to pray with the team before they played their games and sow seeds of the Word of God. In 2019, the softball team made the final four in the state tournament. After she finished playing softball as a senior in high school in 2019, she got saved, and I went to her baptism. After that, I went to everything that was special to her. She was baptized at Horse Creek Baptist Church and it was such a special time in her life and mine!

KIM: In 1997, when my aunt Kim was pregnant and carrying her daughter Yasime, at 5 months gestation her placenta was torn and she began bleeding. She ended up having to stay in the hospital and underwent early labor because of the bleeding. To our surprise, overnight, the bleeding had stopped! It was nothing short of a miracle that the bleeding stopped and she was able to carry her daughter for 9 months! It was during this time that her husband, Bobby, was being called to preach and was running from the calling. He battled and fought with it because he did not want to be a preacher. Needless to say, Bobby ended up in ministry. After Yasmine's birth in 1997, my aunt Kim had her second child, Zoey, in 2000. My two special cousins are like sisters to me and they spend time with me every Friday. We pray with them everyday and they are very special people to me!

MADDIE: I have played softball my entire life and knew Jason from my local church. When I began playing softball in the 6th grade, Jason was always there. Before a softball game one night, Jason had rode with us to the game. When we got there, Jason opened the car door and got out, along with everyone else. Jason did not let me out, so there I was locked in the car. It was a two-door car, and Jason was supposed to have let me out! Here I was stuck in the backseat, until someone came to my rescue! At the region championship and finals he was always there and was the loudest in the stand. When I graduated high school, I kept in touch with Jason and he would pray for me. When I got into

Morehead College in Eastern Kentucky, he called me each week to see how things were going. After a while, he began calling me randomly. This past spring and summer, I was studying for the MCAT, which is a medical college admission test. As I was preparing for it by studying and taking practice tests, my scores were not where I wanted them to be, so I began questioning my path in the Lord. When I was hesitant, Jason would call me, or I would call him. The preparation of this test really humbled me. The MCAT was very mentally and emotionally draining, but Jason kept on encouraging me and told me, "God's got this." The first time I took the MCAT, I failed. Thankfully, Jason would call and encourage me. The second time I took the MCAT, Jason and I prayed while we waited to get the scores. On July 26th I received passing scores in the mail! Unfortunately, on July 28, 2022, my family experienced record breaking rains that flooded our town and we lost our home and all our belongings. Jason kept encouraging me to the plan that God had for me. On August 5, 2022, I got a call for an interview at the University of Kentucky. Jason just knew that I was going to be accepted and become a doctor! He would drill it into me even when I did not believe it. On a Saturday after my interview, Jason called me and I told him about the interview.. Jason kept encouraging me and praying for me to get in. On October 15, 2022, I found out that I got accepted into University of Kentucky's medical school! My dream was to work in rural Kentucky as a doctor and now that can happen! Jason always knew what God's plan was and he always knew what God was going to do in my life. Jason has a connection with God and I am so thankful for him. He is spiritually intact and God is woven into every aspect of Jason's life. Jason is always faithful to God! I am so blessed to have him in my corner and he prays for me each and every day!

DEAN & RUTH: I had known Jason for a while, but we had not spoken but a few times. Jason was preaching at Rockhouse Church on Crane Creek in Oneida, Kentucky. My husband and I decided to go. I was sitting in the church listening to Jason preach and the Lord moved on me to testify about my daughter having had three miscarriages and how emotionally upset we were. Jason and others began praying for me at the altar. Jason began prophesying that my daughter would have a child. From that night forward, Jason called me nightly and prayed for my daughter and my family. I have many notes of prophecy in my Bible from Jason during those nightly calls. I remember specifically Jason saying "This time, this time, this time!" Those words stuck with me and I knew this time things would be different. Jason also called my daughter and prayed with her. At one point, Jason had her come to my house and he prayed with her. He instructed me to have a rocking chair sitting in the middle of the room, and he wanted my daughter to sit in the rocking chair while we prayed for her. He told her she would have her baby, and that it would be soon. About a week later, I was coming home from church when I noticed that I had a missed call from my daughter. When I called her back, she excitedly said, "I'm pregnant!" I called Jason to let him know the good news. My daughter and her husband scheduled a doctor's appointment and asked me to go. Unfortunately, I had to work and was unable to go with them, but of course would be praying for them. In the other pregnancies of my daughter, a heartbeat was not found. I was sitting at my desk at work and my phone began to ding. I looked down and it was a text from my son-in-law. It said, "We have a heartbeat!" I began worshiping God in my office! Not only did we have a heartbeat, it was a strong heartbeat of 160 beats per minute! My daughter ended up having a healthy baby girl. Jason prayed every single day! Several months later, Jason told me she was going to have another baby. I thought he was joking, but he wasn't. When my grandchild was 16-months-old, my daughter had another healthy baby girl. What a wonderful, awesome God we serve!

There was another instance when my son wanted to be a physical therapist. So, I called Jason and we began to pray for my son to get into a physical therapy program. It was extremely difficult to get in the program with over 800 applicants and 20 recipients. At my son's first attempt, he did not get in. Jason told him what he had to do to get in the program. My son did what the Lord wanted. At the next round of applications, my son applied to four different schools. This time, not only did he get accepted into the program of choice, but was accepted into ALL four programs! After he graduated from his program, we began to pray for the Lord to send him the wife God wanted him to have. Shortly after we began praying, he was introduced to the one God would have for him to marry. God sent him a wonderful wife and they are very happy and have a healthy baby girl.

TERAH: Jason is my first cousin and such a blessing in my life. I am originally from Manchester, Kentucky, but moved to Cadiz, Kentucky when I was 5-years-old. The first five years of my life, my aunt Barb (Jason's mother) helped take care of me while my parents worked. Barb was like a second mother to me and has been one of the most influential people in my life. She and Jason have been my prayer warriors and have prayed for so many breakthroughs in my life. By the grace of God, I was able to graduate as salutatorian of my high school graduating class. Then, the Lord placed it on my heart to pursue a career as a nurse practitioner. Through prayer, and the Lord's guidance, He made that dream come true. I married my college sweetheart, Graham, in 2012. We longed to become parents, yet suffered years of infertility, failed treatments, IVF, and loss. After my first miscarriage, the Holy Spirit spoke to me that one day we would have a child. I clung to that promise! The prayers of my family and friends (especially from the outpouring love from Barb and Jason) carried us through. Even though we would endure more heartache along the way, God answered our prayers. On December 27, 2019, our miracle baby boy, Ben, arrived. We praise God for being with us through the storms in our life and for allowing our trials to help strengthen our faith and give glory to Him. 1 Peter 1:6-7 says, "So be truly glad. There is wonderful joy ahead, even though you must endure trials for a little while. These trials will show that your faith is genuine. It is being tested as fire tests and purifies gold, though your faith is more precious than mere gold. So when your faith remains strong through many trials, it will bring you much praise and glory and honor on the day when Jesus Christ is revealed to the whole world."

RICHARD & JACKLYNN: I had known Richard and Jacklynn for some time and was invited to their wedding in 2013. We had been going to the same church for about a year, so I had gotten to know them quite well. From 2013 to 2018 we talked some, but not often. In 2018, the Lord impressed upon me to get in touch with them and to pray for them. I had no idea what to do, but I wanted to be obedient. When I contacted them, they shared with me that they wanted to have a child. I went to their home and prayed with them. Nothing happened. Shortly after, they decided they were going to adopt a child instead. On the day the papers would be signed to go forward with the adoption, Jacklynn finds out that she is pregnant.She and her husband now have two children of their own!

JILL: In 2018, I was coming out of a church service when a lady met me outside who had been listening to me preach through the radio ministry. I asked her if there was anything I could pray with her about. She gave me her name and number and I began calling her weekly. In 2019, her niece Elizabeth was in need of prayer. I prayed and fasted for 40 days about this situation for Elizabeth. Between 2019 and 2020, God moved! At this time, Elizabeth began calling me for prayer, and we have become really good friends. In the beginning months of 2021, Elizabeth called me and said, "Guess what?" I replied, "You're pregnant!" Sure enough she was! I was able to get to be a part of Elizabeth's baby dedication in 2021, the Saturday before Mother's Day. When my mommy died, Elizabeth sent me a wind chime that is now at the entrance of my home. It is a great reminder of our friendship!

THOMASA: In 2017, my friend, Thomasa, attended the Women's Mountain Retreat in Pigeon Forge, Tennessee. When she returned from that trip, she said she felt the Lord the entire three day event. She asked me to go with her the next time the event occurred. Although I never really had plans on going, God did. Kyla Rowland, the lady that hosts the event, is a songwriter. She has written the song, "The wall of prayer." In January 2018, God laid it on my heart to call Kyla, but I really did not want to. Sometimes when God puts things on our hearts to do, we are often hesitant for various reasons. One excuse was that I did not have Kyla's phone number. When I called Thomasa later on, to my surprise, she had Kyla's phone number. Now, I don't have any excuses anymore! I called Kyla and told her what God had spoken to me about her, in relation to the book of Job. I began to tell Kyla how she had felt like Job for the past several years. While sharing this with her, she began crying, shouting and praising the Lord! After our conversation, she asked me to come to the Women's Mountain Retreat and pray before the service in August 2018. I agreed, and on the way to the event, Kyla's assistant, Glenna called me and said that I would be praying the Saturday morning before the event was dismissed. Glenna said there would be a lot of people there with cancer that were seeking healing from the Lord. I was really nervous because I would be praying over a lot of sick people, and I wanted God to move for them. After the event was over, I became good friends with Kyla and Glenna.

GAIL: While at the Women's Mountain Retreat, I met a woman named Gail. Gail had cancer. She wanted my phone number so I could pray with her more often. I began calling her weekly and praying with her. I prayed with her every week until the cancer became severe, then I began calling and praying with her daily, and did so until she went home to be with the Lord. Gail loved my mommy. Gail would call my mommy 'Momma Root'. Mommy would cry every time she talked to Gail. Gail would pray for me and my family and that touched my mommy to tears. When I would do Facebook Lives, Gail wanted to see my face, so she purchased and mailed me a tripod for my device. Gail encouraged me to set up the tripod and now I use it every time I go live.

KAREN: At the first of the year in 2019, God wanted me to call a woman named Karen. She was the Commonwealth Attorney for Bell Co, Kentucky. Again, this was one of those things that I did not want to do, but God insisted and made a way by providing me with her phone number. I called Thomasa and of course she had the phone number and come to find out, was good friends with Karen. I called Karen and prayed with her, and God moved in the situation that needed a solution. I did not know at the time that she was Matt Jones' mother, who was at the time over Kentucky Sports Radio. I listened to Kentucky Sports Radio and was a huge fan. When Karen shared a situation that her son,

Matt, was battling, I began praying and fasting for him to make the right decision. I was blessed to meet him at his mother's house and pray with him after he finished recording one of his radio shows. God moved in this situation, and he has put a testimony about me in a book that he wrote called, "Mitch, Please!." After Matt wrote that book, I felt led by the Lord to write my own and share what wonderful things God has done for me and my life.

RODNEY & TABITHA: At the end of 2020, I went to my friend's Rodney and Tabitha's house and prayed with them. They had a little girl named Addie, but wanted more children. Tabitha struggled to get pregnant with her first child, Addie. Because of Tabitha's age and other complications from before, they knew they needed to pray before trying a second time. So we prayed about that and Tabitha and her sister-in-law, Ashley became pregnant at the same time!

KENDRA: In 2015 God helped me to meet a lady by the name of Kendra. She was 25-years-old when I met her. The day I met her, I had no idea that she did not have any gas money. God spoke to me and told me to give her $20. I didn't know why God spoke to me, so I just did it. Since then, God has blessed her to run a successful t-shirt shop called Pearl Apparel in London, Kentucky. By prayer, I knew that God would bless her business. Prior to her shop opening, she and I dedicated it to the Lord. She is a great Christian lady.

ALICIA: The song leader at Binghamtown Baptist Church asked me if I would start praying with Alicia over the phone. Alicia was a member of that church. After the first time I called her, she asked if I would call her back and pray with her daily. I ended up calling her everyday for about two years! Alicia had been diagnosed with stomach cancer, and at one point was in a coma for an extended period of time. I had been in intensive prayer for her healing prior to her going into a coma. I was so blessed when I got the phone call that she came out of the coma! When she came out of the coma, she said God visited her and had told her that Jason (I) had "fixed up her healing" all because I had prayed for her! When Alicia came out of the coma she shared her testimony of the visitation from the Lord with all the nurses that were caring for her at the hospital. One nurse in particular gave her life to the Lord because of Alicia's testimony! Sadly, two weeks later, I received a phone call that Alicia went home to be with the Lord. She was the most special person that I ever prayed for. I was so very close to her and it was devastating to lose her. It was very hard to lose her, but I know she is with Jesus now and fully healed.

~11~ Dependent on God 100%

Isaiah 41:13 "For I the Lord thy God will hold thy right hand, saying unto thee, Fear not; I will help thee."

When I had 20/20 vision (with glasses), I trusted what I could see. I did not have to depend on anyone or anything. Since losing my vision, I now have to depend on God and others to help me. I thank God that He has put the right people in my life to help me and love me. Even when I had vision, I still had to depend on God to bring me through difficult situations. In high school, I wore glasses, but when I was given tests in small print, I struggled to read them. I would pray and ask God to help me so I could pass, and He did every time! I was able to graduate from high school without failing a class or having to attend summer school.

In 1993, I was a sophomore in high school. It was in that year that my father was injured at work, and my mother had just bought a new vehicle. Of course with a new vehicle came a car payment each month. This vehicle was financed for 6 years! When my father hurt his back by shoveling coal into one of the train carts, he was no longer able to work. He received some pay for sick-leave through worker's compensation, however it was not enough to pay bills and make a new car payment. My parents were seeking after worker's compensation, due to the loss of pay from being injured on the job. It was a long process and things were getting tight. Inevitably, the car payment lapsed and the vehicle was going to be repossessed. The day it was supposed to be repossessed, a large check came in the mail from worker's compensation and my mother was able to make a year-in-advance payment! This showed me how important it was to depend on God. During the time of financial strain, I learned how to depend on God for everything.

In 1999, my father finally received a VA pension from Agent Orange and my family became even more financially stable.

After my father passed, we faced more challenges that required God's intervention. Some were financial. In 2007, after my father's passing, I remember going to the Social Security Office to notify them of his death, and to sign-up for Social Security benefits. My mother and I prayed before we went in and asked God to send us an angel for help. So, we went in, sat down, and waited for our turn. When our turn came, surprisingly, a lovely lady assisted us and said she would try to help us anyway that she could. After we left there, we said, "God sent us an angel today!" After my father's passing, it took over a year for my mother to receive widow's pay. I continue to get a small amount of income from my father's Social Security. It did not matter though, God provided everything we needed that year and more!

The last five years before my mother passed, she drew even closer to the Lord through deep study of God's Word in reading daily devotions. In October 2021, my mother passed while reading her daily devotion. After my mother passed, I really had to depend even more on God. When she passed, my brother and I lost two-thirds of our monthly income. Even though we have not received any compensation from the VA for the side effects of Agent Orange, the Lord has provided in other ways. The two-thirds we lost, God has doubled since, and we have not gone without anything. I have kept on doing every ministry my mother helped with, except now it is different people. God blessed me before my mother passed. He knew I was going to need people. God put the right individual's in my path, and I established new friendships that I now depend on. There are people that I will not mention, but they know who they are! These people have supplied our financial needs because they are wealthy enough to do so. Before my mother passed, she always took me to my preaching commitments, but now I have dear friends that take me. My cousin Yasmine, comes over every Friday to help me with setting up my tripod for Facebook Lives, she cuts my hair, and cleans my house. Yasmine's sister, Zoe, cuts up prayer cloths that we mail and send to those that need them. Yasmine and Zoe's mother, picks my brother and I up for church on Sundays. If I need something ordered from the internet, I will have whoever I am with at the time order it. About 90% of what I order is for the ministry. Since Shannon has been sick, I have done my best to help him and depend on God for the rest. Before my mother

passed, Shannon was just my brother, but now it is as though I am his caregiver since his health has

deteriorated. I love my brother regardless, and I know that God is working things out for his good and

mine.

In ministry, I have to be fully dependent on God and do what God says. When God

speaks to me about going places and praying for people, especially people I do not know, I depend on

God to speak through me and direct my steps. At times, God will speak a person's name and lay them

on my heart to call and pray with them. God lets me know when I have met a brother or sister in Christ

and we usually become great friends. When I call people I do not know, I naturally get nervous. I want

God to show up in the conversation and speak through me! When people answer the phone that are nice

and receptive, it eases the nervousness. There are those, however, who are not so nice and it can be

heart-breaking when people refuse prayer. I still pray for those people when I hang up the phone,

because that is what God would have me do. I depend on God to do the ministry through me. I am just

a vessel for Him. Writing this book has required me to be dependent on God, not only to help me write

it, but for the words that would go in it. Writing this book has not been an easy task, but doable because

of God's help.

~12~ Side Effects of Agent Orange

According to the U.S. Department of Veteran Affairs (VA) website, Agent Orange was a tactical herbicide that was used during the Vietnam War by the U.S. military to clear leaves and other vegetation for military operations. The VA website claims that the use of Agent Orange may have led to cancers or other illnesses. Although the website claims to offer compensation to those who have been impacted by Agent Orange, the eligibility requirements are qualifying only to individuals with certain stipulations, of which my brother and I do not qualify.

During the Vietnam War, my father was sprayed with a substance called Agent Orange. Once he came home from the war, he began to have side effects that would change his life. At the time of my father's death, he was on about 25 different medications. He went to various doctors monthly, and more frequently as his health deteriorated. The last year and a half of his life, he stayed in and out of the hospital. The last six months of his life, he stayed in a hospital until he passed on. After my father passed, it took my mother over a year to receive widow benefits from the Veterans Affairs Office. My mother did not seek after benefits for my brother and I, because she knew it would be a struggle. My father came home from Vietnam in 1970, but did not start drawing veteran benefits until 1999, even though he had significant health concerns, reports, and operations. It took many years to prove the effects of Agent Orange before the Federal Government would compensate those that were impacted. One of the side effects that took a toll on his mind was post-traumatic stress disorder (PTSD). As a result of PTSD, my father began having nightmares. These nightmares were severe and threatening to those around him. At times, during these episodes, my father would become violent and he would lash out at my brother and I. These episodes were so bad, that my father eventually had to live on his own.

My father also developed diabetes, heart disease, scoliosis, neuropathy, gum disease, gastroparesis, and cirrhosis of the liver. Each of these ailments led to operations, aches and pains that would eventually end his life. The side effects that my brother and I endured, significantly changed our lives in comparison to other children. Both my brother and I have Retinitis Pigmentosa and are blind because of this eye disease. I developed an 8lb nodule on my thyroid that had to be removed in 2015. In the same year, I had kidney stones removed and my gallbladder. Thankfully, it was not cancer! Today, I am on medication for my thyroid and will take it the rest of my life. I also have problems with my teeth and may end up losing a few in time. My brother (who passed in March 2023), had cirrhosis of the liver and was on a transplant list. We praise God that he was healthy enough to be placed on the list and believed that God would bless him with a new liver at the right time. In addition to cirrhosis of the liver, Shannon also had mental deficiencies, neuropathy and difficulties with his esophagus. Although we have state medicaid, we do not receive any financial benefits to compensate for our loss of privileges as a result of Agent Orange. Current law only allows for financial compensation to those born with certain health conditions. With God's help, we have done well and He has blessed us beyond measure. My reason for writing this book is to bring attention to the lack of assistance for those who are impacted by Agent Orange. My brother and I have sought legal means to try and fight this discrepancy, however, we have not had any luck. No political official in Kentucky has offered to help us either. We have given our paperwork to various attorneys, but so far, nothing has progressed. Glory to God for making this book possible, and our prayer is that it would shed light on this issue and those suffering from Agent Orange effects.

At the time of writing this book, my brother, Shannon was 51-years-old and needed around the clock care. We are both blind and require assistance to differing degrees. We have not received any benefits from the VA, but pray that God can and will change that for all those who suffer from similar diseases.

~13~ Where I am Today

Psalms 118:34 "This is the day the Lord has made, let us rejoice and be glad in it."

God has been getting me ready for the new season and year ahead. I am still working for the Lord and preaching when God opens the door. I still pray for people on the phone everyday. We are going into a new year in just a few weeks (2023). God has a new vision for the church in the new year. The Bible says that without a vision the people perish (Proverbs 29:18). I feel as though it is time to do more outside of the walls of the church. God is calling us outside of the church to work and expand in prayer and preaching. In 2020, I began sending people packages in the mail that contained crosses and prayer cloths. In 2023, I am going to start putting small Bibles in them and expanding on my mail ministry as God provides.

As for my prayer ministry, I recently prayed for a man on the phone who was in need of a lung transplant. Just a few days later, he was blessed to have a 15-hour surgery for a lung transplant! I praise God for that! I am praying for my cousin, Terah, to have more children, and believing God she will conceive once again. I am also praying for a close friend and his deliverance from the bondage of addiction. Even though God has not delivered him today, I believe God will do it tomorrow! I pray over businesses and dedicate buildings to the Lord. I have a radio and podcast ministry and I do Facebook Lives everyday for those that need prayer. I have baptized 15 people since I began preaching. I have done baby dedications and even married four couples, three of which are still married! Praise God! I still lead people to Jesus and follow-up with them to make sure they are still on the right track and attending a local church. I am praying for other things in my life that I need God to move in, and I trust in time He will. I will keep on believing until it happens. Without faith we cannot please God (Hebrews 11:6). God has blessed me going in and coming out each day. His hand of protection has been and will continue to be on me. I am so thankful for God's hand in my life. I have a nursing home ministry where I visit and pray with the elderly every Tuesday night. I even won "Pastor of the Year," in 2020 for ministering in the local nursing home. During COVID we did not quit praying for people in the nursing home. Sometimes we sat in the car and prayed for people. Other times, we walked around the building praying. However we prayed, we did and were obedient to what God was doing there. I currently offer prayer and fellowship at a local drug rehab facility at Chad's Hope in Manchester. I never turn away preaching commitments, and will go wherever the Lord sends me, regardless of denomination.

As for my brother, Shannon, in July 2022, he was diagnosed with stage four cirrhosis of the liver and was placed on a transplant list. He began the process to undergo surgery. Had a liver become available, he wanted to be prepared. When my mother died in October 2021, I began staying more with Shannon at my mother's house. I slept on a couch in another room where I could be close to him, then I began sleeping on a couch next to him as the cirrhosis became more severe. I slept next to Shannon until November 2021, when he began sleeping in a hospital bed. At that time, I began sleeping on a bed in another room. Shannon began retaining fluid as a result of the cirrhosis and his ammonia levels would rise and cause confusion. Shannon made frequent trips to the hospital to have fluid drained off his stomach. In fact, the doctors would drain many liters at one time. In November 2022, Shannon had tests to make sure he would be healthy enough to undergo the transplant surgery. One of the stipulations required having all your teeth pulled, and over a period of several months, Shannon had all his teeth removed. With high ammonia levels and confusion, Shannon often went to the hospital for short stays to be monitored. On the night of Wednesday, March 22, 2023, I stayed with Shannon and I noticed he made odd grunting noises while trying to sleep. He had done this before. Shannon did not like to be bothered while he was sleeping, so I waited until the following morning before I contacted my aunt Faye. A few days earlier, we were eating at the table with bubby (Shannon), and that was the first time in months he had been able to sit at the table and eat with us. There was a three day span where bubby had good days and they were by far the best few days he had in many months. On Thursday, March 23, 2023, we attempted to wake him up to eat breakfast and to take his medications. Shannon would not respond. I screamed at him to the top of my lungs, but he would not wake-up. I knew there was a possibility of him going into a coma, I just did not think it would happen this soon. We called an ambulance and he was transported to the nearest hospital in Manchester. The doctor on staff told us that his ammonia levels were high and were contributing to the coma. Once the levels dropped, the hope was he would come out of it. When his levels went down the next day, Shannon did not wake up. I knew that he would likely not come out of it. We were asked about hospice care, however, he would have to come off the transplant list. It was a hard decision, but we knew it was best. All the doctors said the cirrhosis was a result of Agent Orange.

Shannon went home to be with the Lord on March 25, 2023 at 7:30 a.m., exactly fifteen months after my mother passed away. On Friday morning, prior to Shannon's passing, God spoke to me. I knew it was time for Shannon to go meet Jesus. I knew Shannon could hear me, so I told him to go home and get his healing. Praise God, he did! I know that he is fully healed and no longer suffering from cirrhosis. I will miss him and he was such a good bubby to me.

I will miss my bubby and my mother from now on, but I keep on going and pressing toward the mark (Philippians 3:13-14). My prayer is that God would open doors for those impacted by the effects of Agent Orange, whether in compensation or treatment. This is not just about getting compensated, but shedding light on all those who suffer. They need prayer! After reading this book, I ask that you pray for all those who are impacted by Agent Orange. You may not know these people by name, but God does! He will move in their lives through your prayers for them. Please pray for me also and ask God to continue to provide each step of the way! I am always open to new ideas for ministry to try and reach people for Jesus. We have to be open to what God has for us and His leading. I am always accessible to people via Facebook Messenger under Jason Root. I rejoice in what God has done in my life and what He will continue to do. I will rejoice and be glad for this day the Lord has made (Psalms 118:34)!

NOTES

Agent orange exposure and VA disability compensation. Veterans Affairs. (n.d.). Retrieved March 18, 2023, from
https://www.va.gov/disability/eligibility/hazardous-materials-exposure/agent-orange/

Access your bible from anywhere. BibleGateway.com: A searchable online Bible in over 150 versions and 50 languages. (n.d.). Retrieved March 18, 2023, from
https://www.biblegateway.com/

Made in the USA
Columbia, SC
08 June 2023

17702620R00026